FIRST LOOK

IN THE AIR

For a free color catalog describing Gareth Stevens' list of high-quality children's books, call 1-800-341-3569 (USA) or 1-800-461-9120 (Canada).

Library of Congress Cataloging-in-Publication Data

Llewellyn, Claire.
    First look in the air / Claire Llewellyn.
        p. cm. — (First look)
    "North American edition"—T.p. verso.
    Includes bibliographical references and index.
    Summary: A simple introduction to the properties of air, the types of animals that fly through the air, and the types of aircraft used by people for transportation and fun.
    ISBN 0-8368-0701-4
    1. Air—Juvenile literature. 2. Birds—Flight—Juvenile literature. 3. Flight—Juvenile literature. 4. Airplanes—Juvenile literature. [1. Air. 2. Flight.] I. Title. II. Series.
QC161.2.L54 1991
533'.6—dc20   91-9426

North American edition first published in 1991 by
Gareth Stevens Children's Books
1555 North RiverCenter Drive, Suite 201
Milwaukee, Wisconsin 53212, USA

U.S. edition copyright © 1991 by Gareth Stevens, Inc. First published as *In the Air* in the United Kingdom, copyright © 1991, by Simon & Schuster Young Books. Additional end matter copyright © 1991 by Gareth Stevens, Inc.

Photograph credits: Jean-Paul Ferrero/ARDEA LONDON, 25; ZEFA, all others

Series editor: Patricia Lantier-Sampon
Design: M&M Design Partnership
Cover design: Laurie Shock
Layout: Sharone Burris

Printed in the United States of America

1 2 3 4 5 6 7 8 9 97 96 95 94 93 92 91

FIRST LOOK

CLAIRE LLEWELLYN

IN THE AIR

Gareth Stevens Children's Books
MILWAUKEE

Books in the
FIRST LOOK series:

FIRST LOOK AT
THE AIRPORT

FIRST LOOK AT
BOATS

FIRST LOOK AT
CARS

FIRST LOOK AT
CHANGING SEASONS

FIRST LOOK AT
CLOTHES

FIRST LOOK AT
DAY AND NIGHT

FIRST LOOK IN
THE FOREST

FIRST LOOK AT
GROWING FOOD

FIRST LOOK IN
THE HOSPITAL

FIRST LOOK
IN THE AIR

FIRST LOOK AT
KEEPING WARM

FIRST LOOK AT
MOUNTAINS

FIRST LOOK AT
RIVERS

FIRST LOOK
UNDER THE GROUND

FIRST LOOK
UNDER THE SEA

FIRST LOOK AT
USING ENERGY

CONTENTS

Fun in the Air 6

Wings are Light but Strong 8

Birds are Expert Fliers 10

Flying Insects...12

Flying Is Useful and Exciting 14

Falling through the Air 16

Moving Air 18

A Little Help from the Wind 20

Water in the Air 22

Air Is Important 24

Air Pollution...26

Fun on the Ground 28

More Books about Air 30

Glossary 30

Index..32

FUN IN THE AIR

Do you like to play on a swing? Do you like going high? Is it scary? Is it fun? Do you feel heavy or light?

How does the air feel on your face?

How do you think it feels to fly?

7

WINGS ARE LIGHT BUT STRONG

Bats and birds have hollow bones in their wings. This helps them fly because the bones don't weigh a lot.

Have you ever seen a bat? At what time of day did you see it?

How are a bat's wings different from a bird's?

BIRDS ARE EXPERT FLIERS

How do birds use their wings to fly?

Some birds have long, large wings. Other birds have short, tiny wings.

Do all birds use their wings in the same way?

11

FLYING INSECTS

Most insects can fly. Can you name some?

How many wings do the insects in these pictures each have?

Two of the ladybug's wings are hard. How do you think this helps it fly?

FLYING IS USEFUL AND EXCITING

Many people enjoy flying. Can you think of some reasons why?

Since people don't have wings, they build special flying machines.

Do you know the names of the machines in these pictures? How are they different from each other?

15

FALLING THROUGH THE AIR

Have you ever dropped something like an egg, a cup, or a bottle of milk? Were you able to catch it in time?

A parachute helps things fall through the air slowly so they can land safely. How do you think it works?

When might a parachute be useful?

MOVING AIR

Wind is air that moves. Which way is the wind blowing in the picture?

Some winds can be very strong. Hurricanes are the strongest. Can you name some other strong winds?

A LITTLE HELP FROM THE WIND

Look at the dandelion in the picture below.
What will happen to it when the wind blows?
How does this help the dandelion?

What other plants does the wind help?

The wind helps people, too. Can you think of
some ways?

WATER IN THE AIR

There is water in the air. This water is in such tiny drops that we cannot see it most of the time. It is invisible — like air itself.

Do you know where water in the air comes from? Can you think of times when you are able to see it?

23

AIR IS IMPORTANT

Insects, other animals, and plants breathe in different ways, but they all need air to stay alive. Can you guess where worms and fish find air to breathe?

Have you ever had a hard time catching your breath? When? What did it feel like?

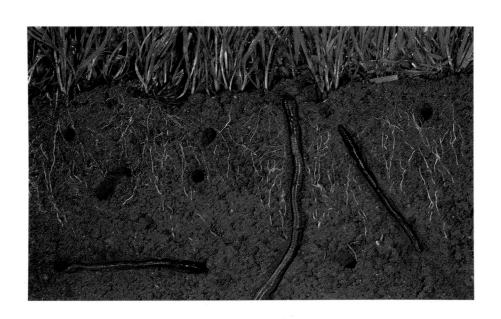

AIR POLLUTION

Look at these pictures. Every day we pollute the air in many different ways. What do you think pollution smells like?

How can we stop or prevent some kinds of air pollution?

What do you think happens to the tiny insects and plants in places where the air is badly polluted?

27

FUN ON THE GROUND

What is inside this balloon and these
bubbles? Where did it come from?
How did it get there?

Can you think of any other ways that
children and grown-ups use air to have fun?

29

More Books about Air

Air. Averous (Silver Burdett)
Air. Brandt (Troll Associates)
Air. Parramon (Barron's Educational Series)
Air. Webb (Franklin Watts)
Air, Air, Air. Jefferies (Troll Associates)
Air is All Around You. Branley (Harper & Row Junior Books)
In the Air. Booth (Raintree)
In the Air. Fitzpatrick (Silver Burdett)
Oxygen Keeps You Alive. Branley (Harper & Row Junior Books)
Pollution and Conservation. Lambert (Franklin Watts)
Up in the Air. Livingstone (Holiday House)

Glossary

Bats: Small mammals that can fly. Bats have furry bodies, and they fly mostly at night.

Breathe: To take air in and then send it back out again. Plants, animals, and people all have a breathing process.

Dandelions: Plants that have bright yellow flowers and large, green leaves. Dandelions are a type of weed.

Hollow: Empty on the inside. Bats' bones are hollow. This helps them fly more easily.

Hurricanes: Storms with very strong winds that usually begin in tropical areas. Hurricane winds reach speeds of at least 75 miles (120 km) per hour.

Insects: A group of animals each having six legs and a body that is divided into three parts. Most insects also have wings. Butterflies, grasshoppers, and bees are examples of insects.

Invisible: Hidden from sight or view. The droplets of water in the air are invisible most of the time.

Ladybugs: Little beetles that are usually red, orange, or yellow in color with black spots. Ladybugs eat insects that can harm plants.

Parachute: A large piece of cloth folded into a pack that is strapped to the back of a sky diver or to anything that is thrown out of an airplane or helicopter. An open parachute is umbrella-shaped and catches air so that the person or object falling slows down.

Pollute: To make something dirty. Both gasoline exhaust from cars and trucks and cigarette smoke cause air pollution.

Wind: Air that moves. A strong wind can help run a windmill or make a balloon fly.

Index

A number that is in **boldface** type means that the page has a picture of the subject on it.

airplanes **15**, **27**

bats **8**, 9
birds 9, 10-**11**
breathing 25
butterflies **13**

dandelions **21**

flying machines 14-**15**

helicopters **15**
hurricanes 18

insects **12-13**, 25, 26

ladybugs **12**, 13

parachutes **16**, 17
plants 25, 26
pollution 26-**27**

swing 6, **7**

water 22-**23**
wind 18-**19**, 20-21
windmills **20**
wings: artificial 14, **15**, **27**;
    natural **8**-9, 10, **11**, **12**, **13**